Lord Montagu

Expostulation in Extremis : or, Remarks on Mr. Gladstone's

Lord Montagu

Expostulation in Extremis : or, Remarks on Mr. Gladstone's

ISBN/EAN: 9783337079178

Printed in Europe, USA, Canada, Australia, Japan

Cover: Foto ©ninafisch / pixelio.de

More available books at **www.hansebooks.com**

EXPOSTULATION IN EXTREMIS:

OR,

REMARKS ON MR. GLADSTONE'S

"POLITICAL EXPOSTULATION

ON THE

VATICAN DECREES

IN THEIR BEARING ON

CIVIL ALLEGIANCE."

BY THE RIGHT HON. LORD ROBERT MONTAGU, M.P.

"Although I hit you first, yet it is no matter; I will have an action of battery against you if there is any law in Illyria."—(Mr. GLADSTONE, *in the part of Sir Andrew Ague-Cheek*).

London:

BURNS & OATES, PORTMAN STREET.

- 1874.

LONDON:

PRINTED BY WHITEHEAD, MORRIS & LOWE,

167 & 168, FENCHURCH STREET, E.C.

EXPOSTULATION IN EXTREMIS.

Mr. GLADSTONE wrote an article in the October number of the *Contemporary Review*, which has, of course, acquired a world-wide celebrity,—or notoriety. In that article (as he himself says in his recent *" Political Expostulation "*), he " did not scruple to use language" which naturally offended many of his friends and supporters. There arose against it a whirlwind of abuse; as there arose a tempest against the prophet Jonah, when he endeavoured to run away from his duty. It speedily became "plain that, in some quarters, his words gave deep offence; displeasure, indignation, and even fury might be said to have marked"[1] their perusal. " More than one friend " *expostulated.* He therefore "proposes (in the "Political Expostulation") to *expostulate* in his turn."[2]   Does he withdraw, or at least · explain away and soften down, the offensive and insulting passages ? No; he says : " I am not, in any particular, disposed to recede ;" he will not even " re-cast their general form ;" he repeats them twice over.[3]

When the surprise, excited on reading such an Expostulation, had somewhat abated, I was led to ask myself the question : Why, in the name of Heaven, did Mr. Gladstone write it at all ? The Expostulation, we must remember, is addressed " to my

---

[1] Political Expostulation, p. 8.   [2] p. 7.   [3] p. 6, p. 12.

Roman Catholic fellow-countrymen."[1] He "conveys an appeal to the understandings of my Roman Catholic fellow countrymen."[2] Why then did he address or "convey" such an appeal and Expostulation to them ? They were indignant and full of "fury" at his former effusion. Did he pen this one in order,—while proving, in justification, the truth of his assertions,—to remove the feeling of soreness which he had incautiously raised in the minds of his "five millions (or nearly one-sixth of the inhabitants of the United Kingdom) of Roman Catholic fellow-countrymen?"[3] Doubtless he inadvertently offended them, and hastened to remove the baneful impression by a dexterous use of Gladstonian rhetoric, and an astute Palmerstonian manipulation of their passions ? But, then, why did he multiply those insults, and give his fellow-countrymen still more "deep offence," and a greater ground for "displeasure, indignation, and even fury?" He asserts[4] that "brain-power" "had been devoted, for centuries, to the single purpose of working into the practice of Christendom, the theory which placed every human being, in things spiritual and things temporal, at the feet of the Roman Pontiff." He speaks of[5] "the shallow policy, vainly used to hide the daring of that wild ambition which, at Rome, not from the throne but from behind the throne, prompts the movements of the Vatican;" as if the supreme Pontiff were a puppet in the hands of a low and dark intriguer! Lest this hardy assertion should escape the notice of some of his "Roman Catholic fellow-countrymen," he repeats it a little lower down on the same page. Presently[6] he puts the same idea in another form, and tells us of "the astute contrivers of this tangled scheme (*i.e.* the Definition of Infallibility,)" and[7] of "the subserviency or pliability of the Council." Again[8] the Vatican decrees are called "this new version of the principles of the Papal Church," which "inexorably binds its

---

members to the admission of these exorbitant claims without any refuge or reservation, &c." We are in the next place given to understand[1] that His Holiness "imitates the flashes of Jove, and moans like the thunder of Olympus." It is all that dogma of the Infallibility of the Head of the Church which riles him,—that[2] "formidable demand for power of the vulgar kind," that[3] "daring raid upon the civil sphere." The Church, he tells us,[4] "is tainted in its views," and is "like an actor who has to perform several characters in one piece."[5] Again we hear[6] of "the myrmidons of the Apostolic Chamber," and[7] the "revolutionary measures of 1870." If the "Roman Catholic fellow-countrymen" were in a "fury" before, what must they feel now? Clearly he cares not for their goodwill.

Then why was the Expostulation penned? Was it an insidious attempt to promote a Döllingerian separation between the people and the Hierarchy? Warrant for this assumption seems to be given, partly by his warm admiration for the heresiarch, which he betrays by a certain tenderness;[8] and partly by the fact of a prolonged visit which Mr. Gladstone has just paid him in the city of pictures and ballet-dancers. This assumption gathers strength on reading the following passages in the "Expostulation."[9] "I shall strive to show to such of my Roman Catholic fellow-subjects as may kindly give me a hearing, that after the singular steps which the authorities of their Church have, in these last years, thought fit to take, the people of this country who fully believe in their loyalty are entitled, on purely civil grounds, to expect from them some declaration or manifestation of opinion, in reply to that Ecclesiastical party in their Church who have laid down, in their name, principles adverse to the purity and integrity of civil allegiance." He then suggests to the Roman Catholic Laity that they should not feel assailed or

---

[1] p. 47.   [2] p. 47.   [3] p. 48.   [4] p. 61.   [5] p. 61.
[6] p. 65.   [7] p. 64.   [8] p. 21.   [9] p. 7.

insulted[1] by " free and strong animadversion on the conduct of
the Papal chair and its advisers and abettors," because they (the
laity) " do not choose their Ecclesiastical rulers, and are not
recognised as having any voice in the government of their
Church,"—which voice they doubtless will have when Mr. Gladstone becomes a British Bismarck, and Falck laws are passed by
a " servile or pliable" House of Commons. This absurd idea of
the sovereignty of the people in Ecclesiastical affairs runs,
indeed, through the whole of the pamphlet ; he even imagines
that there is a " Constitutional Party "[2] in the Church, answering,
no doubt, to the Liberal Party in the State, of which he is the
distinguished head and brilliant ornament. Again he says, [3] " I
feel sincerely how much hardships their (*i.e.* the " quiet-minded
Roman Catholics ") case entails; but this hardship is brought
upon them altogether by the conduct of the authorities of their
own Church."   Those authorities of the Church, from whom he
desires to separate the people, next receive a blow in an epithet,—
[4] " the degradation of the Episcopal Order."   In speaking of the
opinion that the State has no superior (which he regards as
generally upheld), he says, [5] " So it is, I believe, with the mass of
Roman Catholics individually; but not so with the leaders of the
Church."   No ! those leaders are too degraded ! Yet they are
not without ambition : for [6] " individual servitude, however abject,
will not satisfy the party now dominant in the Latin Church."
What is that abject servitude ? Let him explain : he asserts
that, by the definition of the dogma of infallibility, the religion
of every Roman Catholic " has been changed for him over his
head, and without the very least of his participation."   " My
conviction is that, even of those who may not shake off the yoke,
multitudes will vindicate at any rate their loyalty," [7] and he
implores every one not to " forfeit his moral and mental freedom

---

[1] p. 9.   [2] p. 58.   [3] p. 9.   [4] p. 32   [5] p. 10.
            [6] p. 40.   [7] p. 22.

and to place his loyalty and civil duty at the mercy of another (*i.e.*, the Head of the Church)."[1] He also desires us to "repel and reject" the claims of the Pope, and the definitions of the Vatican;[2] and says, that our "Ecclesiastical Rulers" have "acted autocratically";—again the notion of a "Constitutional Party" bewilders him, and buzzes round his mind like a brainfly! It seems, then, that Mr. Gladstone is aiming at a Döllingerian schism, in which he is to act both of the chief parts at once,— that of Döllinger, and that of Bismarck. Yet if this were the aim of the pamphlet, he surely would not hint at the reimposition of the penal laws on the laity for the sins of the hierarchy.

Why, then, did Mr. Gladstone write the Expostulation? Is this "daring raid" made by the sensitive ex-premier as a revenge for the fate of his "University (Ireland) Bill in 1873," and his failure in trying "to give Ireland all that justice could demand?" "When Parliament" he says[3] "had passed the Church Act of 1869 and the Land Act of 1870, there remained only, under the great head of Imperial equity, one serious question to be dealt with—that of higher Education." These were the "three branches" of "the Upas tree of Protestant ascendancy," which he had pledged himself to cut down. He adds in a voice of warning and of sorrow, "The Roman Catholic Prelacy of Ireland thought fit to procure the rejection of that measure . . . . . by the temptation which they thus offered,—the bid, in effect (to use a homely phrase) they made, to attract the support of the Tory opposition."[4] The Tory majority of 1874 is, then, to be visited on the Hierarchy of the Eternal Church!

Yet, No! That cannot be the cause of the Expostulation; for he adds[5] "I consider that the Liberal majority in the House of Commons . . . . . . formally tendered payment in full . . . . by the Irish University Bill of February, 1873;" and [6] "the debt to Ireland has been paid." No one quarrels with a creditor who gives a receipt in full of all demands, without requiring the cash to be handed over! Therefore, this cannot be the cause of the wonderful effusion.

Perhaps it is only an artful and unworthy dodge to unite the Liberal party, and so facilitate his own return to power? One portion of his pamphlet seems to lead to this conclusion. He asks whether his propositions are "material,"—that is, of importance. In what respect? Doubtless it means, material to the safety and welfare of the country, and, as leading to that desirable result, material to the rehabilitation and strength of the Liberal party. He almost informs us of this: [1] "So that while (as I think) general justice to society required that these things which I have now set forth should be written, special justice, as towards the party to which I am loyally attached, and which I may have had a share in thus placing at a disadvantage before our countrymen, made it, to say the least, becoming that I should not shrink from writing them." Material, then, to the great Liberal party, and material to the influence of its great and world-famous leader, and to his chances of returning to the Premier-ship.

But then he says,[2] in answer to the self-suggested question: "Are they (his observations) a recantation and a regret?"—"My reply shall be succinct and plain. Of what the Liberal party has accomplished, by word or deed, in establishing the full civil equality of Roman Catholics, I regret nothing, and I recant nothing." Again:[3] "What, then, is to be our course of policy hereafter? First, let me say that, as regards the great Imperial settlement, achieved by slow degrees, which has admitted men of all creeds subsisting among us to Parliament, that I conceive to be so determined beyond all doubt or question, as to have become one of the deep foundation-stones of the existing Constitution . . . But, if the arguments I have here offered make it my duty to declare

---

[1] p. 56.   [2] p. 61.   [3] p. 63.

them *(sic)*, I say at once, the future will be exactly as the past." If all this storm, which Mr. Gladstone was raising, was "material," then surely it betokened a serious change of policy which would brook no delay,—nay, not so much as would have been necessary to have properly corrected the letter-press of his Expostulation, and expunge a few obvious errors which now deface it. But if nothing is to be changed, why make all this clamour? For the Liberal party, forsooth! Mr. Gladstone had boldly disestablished one Church,—the Irish, but Mr. Disraeli has outdone him this year by undermining the foundation of two Churches—the Scotch and the English. 'What shall I do,' says Mr. Gladstone, 'I must make another bid at this stupendous political auction, and 'expostulate' with the Vatican. Disraeli has professed to put down Ritualism, so I must extinguish Infallibility or crush the Eternal Church!' Will it be knocked down to him? or is he vainly kicking against the pricks?—Surely he would not run his head against a brick wall. This cannot be the aim of the pamphlet.

Lastly: Can it be that Mr. Gladstone imagines that he sees a danger in the Syllabus of December 8th, 1864, and in the Vatican decrees of 1870? The Syllabus was merely a collection of condemnations of propositions,—which condemnations had been passed at anterior dates. We are, therefore, fully warranted in putting the Syllabus aside. It was not a cause of sudden terror to Mr. Gladstone. But Mr. Gladstone explicitly alleges that the Vatican decrees are the origin of his diatribe, just as Bismarck adduced them in justification of the Falck Laws. He says[1]: "I am no longer able to say, as I would have said before 1870, 'There is nothing in the necessary belief of the Roman Catholic which can appear to impeach his full civil title; for whatsoever be the follies of ecclesiastical power in his Church, his Church itself has not required of him, with binding authority,

---

[1] p. 63.

to assent to any principles inconsistent with his civil duty.'
That ground is now, for the present at least, cut from under my
feet." Again : [1] "This daring raid (of 1870) . . . . goes
to the creation of political strife, and to dangers of the most
material and tangible kind. The struggle now proceeding in
Germany at once occurs to the mind as a palmary instance. . .
It is not Prussia alone that is touched; elsewhere the bone
lies ready, though the contention may be delayed." Mr. Gladstone
has got before his mental vision a fight between two curs, over
a bone of contention so gnawed as not to be worth the fighting
Who are the curs ? Bismarck, in Prussia, is of course one.
Who is bidding for that office in England ? Mr. Gladstone
himself. To proceed with the quotation : "In other States, in
Austria particularly, there are recent laws in force, raising much
the same issues as the Falck Laws have raised. . . . . If
I have truly represented the claims promulgated from the
Vatican, it is difficult to deny that those claims, and the power
which has made them, are primarily responsible for the pains
and perils, whatever they may be, of the present conflict between
German and Roman enactments."

Is this fear groundless, or is it a sufficient justification for the
charges contained, and the penal legislation broadly hinted at, in
Mr. Gladstone's pamphlet ? Why, these very doctrines have
been held and taught for many centuries (although not as an
article of faith and necessary to salvation) by all the eminent
doctors of the Church. All Catholics held from the first, and
were bound to hold, that the gift of Infallibility was inherent in
the Church, and was exercised by the Teaching Body of the
Church, including the Pope, in all matters relating to Faith and
morals. The Vatican decrees merely asserted that this Infallibility
of the Church was exercised through her Head, when he spoke
officially as such. Moreover, the Bull "*Unam Sanctam*," which

---

[1] p. 48.

contains much more to raise Mr. Gladstone's fears than all the Vatican decrees, has been an article of faith since the year 1302, having been promulgated by and in a Council at Rome. It concludes in these words: *"Subesse Romano Pontefici, omni creaturæ humanæ, declaramus, dicimus, definimus et pronuntiamus omnino esse de necessitate salutis."* This Bull defined the essential, and therefore eternal, relations between Church and State. It was promulgated in full Council at Rome, on Nov. 18, 1302. It was solemnly renewed and confirmed by Pope Leo X., in the 11th Session of the 5th Lateran Council, by the Bull *"Pastor Æternus,"* which says: "Since it is necessary to salvation that all the faithful in Jesus Christ should be in submission to the Roman Pontiff, as the Holy Scriptures and the testimony of the Holy Fathers teach us, and as the constitution *Unam Sanctam* of our predecessor Boniface VIII. declares, we, in our concern for the salvation of souls, for the supreme authority of the Roman Pontiff, and of the Holy See, and for the unity and power of the Church, the Spouse of Jesus Christ, renew and approve this constitution, in accordance with the approbation of the present Holy Council."[1] Both these Bulls are part of the Canon Law. Moreover, S. Bernard and Hugo de Saint-Victor used nearly the same words. Suarez, also, says that the acceptance of the *Unam Sanctam* is necessary to salvation, and that it explicitly declares that the Church holds not only the spiritual, but also the material sword.[2] So does Bellarmine; others also do so, who are too numerous to rehearse. In short we have a concourse of ancient testimony in favour of the *indirect* power of the Supreme Pontiff over temporal affairs. Mr. Gladstone knew this; for he speaks[3] of its being "the peculiarity of Roman theology to thrust itself into the temporal domain." Moreover, Mr. Gladstone gives examples of the actions of Popes in "invading the rights of Princes," viz., Gregory VII., Innocent III.,

---

[1] Sept. Decr. III. tit. vii. de Conciliis.   [2] De Fide Disp. xx.   [3] p. 9.

Paul III., and Pius V.; and those claims he denominates "mummies picked out of Egyptian sarcophagi." [1]   Those claims Mr. Gladstone, therefore, knew to be very ancient.   How then could the allegiance of Englishmen be affected by the decrees of 1870 ?

Perhaps Mr. Gladstone will point, in answer, to a choice expression, which is very likely to be soothing to the "Roman Catholic fellow-countrymen," whom he addresses : [2] "The fangs of the Mediæval Popedom have been drawn, and its claws torn away."   Fangs and claws !   As much as to say that the Holy Church is the Beast of the Apocalypse !   How refreshed Dr. Cumming, Mr. Newdegate, and Mr. Whalley must be with their neophyte !   Yes, Mr. Gladstone means that the decrees of 1870 have served to " refurbish and parade anew every rusty tool she (the Church) was fondly thought to have disused." [3]

Well, but one of the charges which Mr. Gladstone brings against the Church, in order to justify his sweeping accusations, is that she has renounced "the proud boast of *semper eadem.*" What he censures as the *fons et origo mali* is, that she has not continued to be the same as she was in the middle ages ; so that he has on that account just cause for apprehension.   Cause for apprehension ?   Have you not just told us that " her fangs have been drawn, and her claws torn away ? "   You mean, then, that she is powerless for evil !   Why then this sudden panic ?   this childish tremor ?   this insane fear ?   this infantile trepidation at the bugaboos of your brain ?

But if there is any cause of fear, why is it that Mr. Gladstone, who was Premier from 1869 to 1874, and, as such, knew all the secrets of courts and cabinets, and was in a position to forecast events, and who read, surely, all the fearful vaticinations and denunciations of Janus,—of his friend Lord Acton, and of Döllinger & Co.,—why on earth did he, that powerful Premier with an overwhelming Liberal majority at his back, and with

---

Newdegate looking at him,—why did he not do something to protect us? He was then responsible for the safety of the Empire! Did he propose any means to curb "the exorbitancies of Papal assumption?"[1] Why did he not, with that army of mighty paid Ambassadors at his command, procure the rejection of those decrees which were "arbitrary and wilful," that[2] "moral murder," that "stifling of conscience and conviction?"[3]

What did he do while those Vatican decrees were being passed, or when they had been passed? Let us rehearse the great measures which are a halo of glory round his brow. He proposed to cut down "the Upas tree of Protestant ascendancy;" he promised to govern Catholic Ireland in accordance with Irish ideas; he abolished the Irish Protestant Church; he attempted to pass a measure of Higher Education, which, he said, should amply satisfy the desire of Catholics.

Let us cast our glances further back. All Mr. Gladstone's life has been spent in smoothing down the unfortunate religious antagonisms which exist between Her Majesty's subjects. Do we forget the noble part which he took against that iniquitous Ecclesiastical Titles Act? How he opposed it manfully, when he had to tread the wine-press almost alone, and there were but few to help and support him! Do we not recall the part which he took in regard to those oaths which were imposed on Members of Parliament, with a view of excluding Catholics from the Legislature! Has his attitude, when he so bravely set himself against the torrent of passion in the aroused English nation, and their hasty desire to commit injustice on Catholics,—has that attitude wholly passed from our minds? He was ever on the side of right and good feeling. He always endeavoured to blot from the Statute Book the marks and traces of Protestant alarm, Protestant bitterness, Protestant bigotry. We honour him for this.

---

[1] p. 25.   [2] p. 21.   [3] p. 14.

But, oh! how are the mighty fallen! What, in the name of Heaven, has happened to change him? Can it be the same Gladstone who now wants to reimpose the oath, and make us swear that we "abhor, detest, and abjure as impious and heretical that damnable doctrine and position" which was advanced by Gregory VII., Innocent III., Paul III. and Pius V.; and, above all, by Boniface VIII. and Leo X., in the Bulls *Unam Sanctam* and *Pastor Œternus?* Can he really, by some vagary of intellect, think it necessary for us to swear that "no foreign Prince, Prelate, State, or Potentate hath or ought to have any jurisdiction, power, pre-eminence, or authority, Ecclesiastical or Spiritual, within these realms?" Yet, how else can we make, as he demands,[1] "Either a demonstration that neither in the name of faith, nor in the name of morals, nor in the name of the government or discipline of the Church, is the Pope of Rome able . . . . . to make any claim upon those who adhere to his communion, of such a nature as can impair the integrity of their civil allegiance—or else: That if and when such a claim is made, it will . . . . . be repelled and rejected?"

What, I ask again, can have happened to cause him to make such a demand? "The Vatican decree," he says.[2] But that was in 1870! Since that time the Supreme Pontiff has been, as it were, dethroned; his kingdom reduced to a garden; all the religious houses in Germany and Italy confiscated; all the Jesuits expelled; Catholic Austria has been prostrated; Catholic France laid in the dust; Spain torn to pieces by the Revolution; Italy sitting on a volcano; Prussia most powerful; a great wave of infidelity passing over Europe; the "fangs have been drawn, and the claws torn away." Is Popery, then, a menace and a danger? Yes! Because Mr. Gladstone is not in power to shield us from danger.

If he were in power, he would doubtless reverse his just and

---

[1] p. 44.   [2] p. 44.

generous policy? No, not a whit! he "regrets nothing and recants nothing of what the Liberal party has accomplished, by word, or deed, in establishing the full equality of Roman Catholics."[1] No! not the opposition to, and final abolition of the obnoxious oath; not the long and dreary war against the Ecclesiastical Titles Bill; not the dis-establishment of the Irish Church; not the offer of the University (Ireland) Bill. No! all such ideas of persecution are utterly alien and repugnant to the generous mind.

Is Popery a menace and a danger? What terrifies him then? I think I heard that a nocturnal sally in force was once terrified by the rising of a cock pheasant, and so the attack proved abortive. Were Mr. Gladstone's nerves unstrung? Was he writing when the witching hour of midnight boomed out with sepulchral tones upon the midnight air, and the graves were yawning and "the obscene bird was clamouring the livelong night."? What terrified him? He was led "to the painful and revolting conclusion that there is a fixed purpose among the secret inspirers of Roman policy to pursue, by the road of force, upon the arrival of any favourable opportunity, the favourite project of re-erecting the terrestrial throne of the Popedom, even if it can only be re-erected on the ashes of the city, and amidst the whitening bones of the people."[2] Just as I said! Yawning graves, and obscene birds! What a pity that he did not yawn too, and go to bed!

But let him proceed! "The bare idea is itself a portentous evil; I do not hesitate to say that it is an incentive to general disturbance; a premium upon European wars." "It is difficult to over-estimate the effect which it might produce in generating and exasperating strife."[3] Indeed! The obscene bird clamours the livelong night! Yet all the while that Mr. Gladstone was in office,—all the time that Mr. Gladstone was a Member of the House of Commons,—

---

[1] p. 61.   [2] p. 50.   [3] p. 50.

the temporal power existed. Yet, the bird did not clamour then ! Why then is the temporal power a danger now ? Since the days of Charlemagne—nay, even before—the temporal power has existed and served to stop many wars, to prevent the effusion of blood, to put down rebellions, to end tyrannies and oppressions, and to harmonize and unite nations (as I showed at length in my lecture in Dublin from which Mr. Gladstone has quoted.) [1] How then can it become a danger when it has ceased to be intact and unassailed ; nay, when it has well nigh ceased to exist altogether ? Perhaps because Mr. Gladstone feels that it is right that it should be again. If a man unjustly seizes my property and holds it, there is danger of a law-suit. While it was in my hands there was no danger of a law-suit. Would Mr. Gladstone say : It is clear that every man's property, once it has been stolen, and that the theft has become a *fait accompli,* shall, by Act of Parliament, be retained by the robber, lest there should otherwise be a danger of law-suits ? I should say that the best way of getting rid of the law-suits would be to restore the property to the rightful owner. But we must make allowances ; Mr. Gladstone was writing after midnight.

Is this, then, the only cause of fear ? or shall we add to it a perception in Mr. Gladstone's mind, that all the persecution in the world, and all the spoliation of the Catholic Church throughout the world, cannot bring her nearer to a grave, and that (to use Mr. Disraeli's grand words on November 9th, 1874) " that immemorial and supernatural throne, which Emperors and Kings had for centuries failed to control," rests upon a divine and eternal rock against which the gates of hell cannot prevail ;—that the Church is as strong or even stronger now that all the Governments of Europe, America, and Asia are arrayed against Her ? Is this the cause of fear, aroused, indeed, by the conversion of one or two of Mr. Gladstone's friends ? Does he fear that

---

[1] " Civilisation and the See of Rome," Dublin, McGlashan and Gill, 50, Upper Sackville Street, 1874.

England is about to rush into the arms of the Papacy? No! he has said[1] " At no time since the bloody reign of Mary has this been possible ;" and he adds that it is still less possible now than it was in the seventeenth and eighteenth centuries, because She has quitted the proud boast of *semper eadem,* which he afterwards explains to mean—" the arbitrary way in which she forced the Vatican decrees, in 1870, on moderate-minded Catholics,"—that is, Liberal-Catholics. Nay ; the conversion of one or two of the nobility cannot frighten one who asserts that " the people cannot be charmed, by any incantation, into the Roman camp."

Let us then cease from trying to unravel " the tangled web " of Mr. Gladstone's mind, or to divine the cause of his writing the present Expostulation. Enough for us to consider the point of the effusion. The primary issue is[2] the substantial truth of his four propositions. The first proposition amounts to a charge that, whereas the Church of Rome used to boast proudly that she was one and unchangeable, she has, in 1870, adopted " a policy of violence and change." The change, he explains to be a " development "[3] of the old doctrine; and, also, merely an addition to the old belief; for the Church, he avers, " maintains what the Mediæval Church maintained." This addition was the " putting opposition out of court " by " the recent decrees of the Vatican."

This Mr. Gladstone terms " the fact,"—the historical fact, which he says, is " most important," as " history is a main pre- servative against all forms both of superstition and unbelief ; "[4] and further he alleges that the Church is " a witness of facts," not " a judge of doctrine."

The Fourth Proposition contains what he calls " the opinion ; " viz : that " the recent Papal decrees are at war with modern thought," and " involve a violent breach with (*sic*) history."[5] Yet he has just told us that there used to be " opposition " to the

---

[1] p. 6.   [2] p. 6, p. 7, p. 12...   [3] p. 13.   [4] p. 13.   [5] p. 14.

B

Church until 1870; that is, as long as the Church, according to his own confession, preserved "an unbroken and absolute identity in belief." Up to 1870, therefore, according to his own account, the thought of the world was at war with the Church. The Church, since 1870, has been, he says, at war with modern thought. So be it then. The same idea was once expressed in simpler language : "the world shall hate you ; " and "happy are ye when men shall persecute you, as they persecuted the prophets before you."

The Second Proposition is, that the Church "has refurbished and paraded anew every rusty tool." These "rusty tools,"[1] Mr. Gladstone explains to be the Propositions of the Syllabus, with which Mr. Gladstone certainly has made very free. Errors, in his edition of them, are numerous, and mis-quotations frequent. But from internal evidence it appears that Mr. Gladstone has received them at second hand, and has not consulted the originals. I will take them seriatim with Mr. Gladstone's numeration.

He says those persons are condemned who "maintain the liberty of the Press." He cites, as his authorities for this state-ment (1) the Encyclical Letter of Pope Gregory XVI. in 1831. Doubtless he means the "Mirari vos" of August 15th, 1832. (2) The Encyclical of Pope Pius IX. Both of these passages refer to bad books and publications: "exscindendâ malorum librorum peste," says Pope Gregory ; and Pope Pius says : "You know very well that, in these times, the haters of all truth and justice and most bitter enemies of our religion, deceiving the people and maliciously lying, disseminating sundry other impious doctrines by means of pestilential books, pamphlets and news-papers, dispersed over the whole world, &c." Surely Mr. Gladstone had not consulted the originals.

The condemned proposition ran as follows : "All citizens have a right to entire, unlimited liberty to manifest and declare

---

[1] p 16 to p. 18.

publicly their thoughts, whatever they may be, by word of mouth, or by the press, or in any other way, and no authority, either ecclesiastical or civil, can put any restriction on that liberty." Does Mr. Gladstone not condemn it too ?—Mr. Gladstone, who repealed the paper duty to ruin " *The Times*," and gagged the press in Ireland by his Peace Preservation and Coercion Acts ?

The authority given for No. 3, is " Syllabus of March 18, 1861, Prop. lxxix." I have never had the advantage of hearing of any Syllabus of that date. But the subject-matter referred to appears in the Syllabus of December 8, 1864, Prop. lxxix. The authorities for No. 5 are given thus—" Syllabus of Pope Pius IX., March 8, 1861," and "Ibid (*i.e.* Syllabus of December 8, 1864), Prop. xix." Clearly Mr. Gladstone is not at home in his authorities ! I have never seen a syllabus of March 8, 1861. Why, moreover, should he translate : " *suis propriis et constantibus juribus sibi a Divino Fundatore collatis*," by the bare expression, " civil rights ? " The same grievous error occurs again at p. 42.

On the same page[1] Mr. Gladstone intercalates some words of his own, which he says must be borne in mind, namely, that Œcumenical Councils are not Œcumenical, because the Church of England (I presume) and the Russo-Greek Church were not therein represented. No; that must be an error of mine; he must sink the Anglican Church. I should not have imputed this to him, unless, indeed, he has never heard of Bulls like the *Unam Sanctam*, which may be said, in his sense, to " have interfered with the jurisdiction of the civil power." Nay, if we go back beyond the Greek schism, we may find that he must also sink the Greeko-Russian Church, on the same ground. Then what becomes of his intercalation, and the " branch theory " which it imports ? He even eats his own words on p. 33, by calling the Council of Trent " a real council." This theory of the independency of Churches is the same principle, which, when applied to con-

---

[1] p. 16.

gregations, results in the dissent called "independency" or "congregationalism." When carried further and applied to individuals, it becomes Quakerism or Spiritualism. Between the Catholic Church and the individualism of ultra-dissent, there is no standing ground; for the one is the affirmation, and the other the negation of the same principle. A denial that the whole Church is one body, one society, a unity, is the same as the assertion of individualism.

But let us return to Mr. Gladstone's edition of the Syllabus: Prop. 7, of which Mr. Gladstone makes so much, will not bear the meaning which he attributes to it. He was, perhaps, unaware that it was taken from the Apostolic letter of August 22, 1851; "*Ad apostolicæ sedis*," which condemned a book called "*Juris Ecclesiastici Institutiones*," by Nutz. If he will be good enough to consult this Apostolic letter, he will find that it means the same as the Bull *Unam Sanctam*, viz.: that the Church has co-active or executive power, (as well as legislative or judicial powers); She may call in the civil arm, or "material sword," in the cause of justice and the interests of order throughout the whole christian commonwealth of nations. The mere short quotation which Mr. Gladstone here gives, and still more the insinuation, p. 42, of "the right to use physical force" is very misleading. He is, indeed, more right when he himself contradicts this assumed meaning, saying,[1] "After all, even in the middle ages, it was not by the direct action of fleets and armies of their own that the Popes contended with Kings who were refractory; it was mainly by interdicts, and by the refusal, which they entailed (*sic*) when the Bishops were not brave enough to refuse their publication, of religious offices to the people."

The next, No. 8, has been somewhat distorted,—not by Mr. Gladstone, I am sure. I charge him only with having incautiously accepted it. The true version runs thus (the words in italics

---

[1] p. 35.

having been omitted by Mr. Gladstone) : " or that a power, not inherent in the office of the Episcopate, *has been* granted to it by the civil authority; *and which* may be withdrawn from it at the discretion of that authority." The next (No. 9) should run thus : " or that *the* immunity of the Church and its ministers *has its origin in* civil right." The same error is made use of, as an argument, on page 42. The 11th and 12th are also not quite correct. The 13th and 14th are thus given by Mr. Gladstone : " or that marriage is not in its essence a sacrament;" " or that marriage not sacramentally contracted has a binding force." The condemned originals are respectively : " The sacrament of marriage is only an accessory to the contract, and separable from it; and the sacrament itself consists in the nuptial benediction alone." "By virtue of a purely civil contract, there may exist, among christians, marriage truly so-called; and it is false that either the contract of marriage among christians is always a sacrament, or that there is no contract if the sacrament be excluded." The latter are · the propositions which were condemned.

We need not dwell further on an incorrectness which, more or less, runs throughout the quotations. They betray what I believe to be the fact, that Mr. Gladstone received them,—and probably his arguments,—from some one across the water, in whom Mr. Gladstone confided a little too much.

Let us turn to Mr. Gladstone's Third Proposition. It is, that every convert to Catholicism must abjure his loyalty. The truth of these four propositions is, he says, the issue that he has brought before us in the " Expostulation." I shall presently turn to the arguments which he advances in support of them. We must first hear the other statements which he has given of the point at issue; as the other statements will serve to elucidate the propositions. His charge is[1] : that " Roman theology thrusts

---

[1] p. 9

itself into the temporal domain." Again :[1] " that the Pope of Rome
had been and was a trespasser upon ground which belonged to
the civil authority, and that he affected to determine by spiritual
prerogative questions of the civil sphere. This fact . . . . .
is the whole and sole cause of the mischiefs. To this fact, and to
this fact alone, my language is referable." This fact, he says
moreover, is a peculiarity of the Catholic Church, which dis-
tinguishes it from every other religious body. Before concluding,
we may consider whether this mark or token is not a proof that
the Catholic Church is *the* Church of Christ, excluding the
" Orientals, Lutherans, Calvinists, Presbyterians, Episcopalians,
Noncomformists, one and all."[2] Again, he states the issue in
this form :[3] " The Rome of the Middle Ages claimed universal
monarchy; the modern Church of Rome has abandoned nothing,
retracted nothing." Again; the point at issue is, " a strict ex-
amination as respects the compatibility of the Vatican decrees
with civil right, and the obedience of subjects."[4] Perhaps
Mr. Gladstone is not aware that it has been,—ever since the days
of the *Unam Sanctam* in 1302, at least,—an article of faith that
the prophecy of Jeremiah :. " Lo, I have set thee this day over
the nations and over the kingdoms to root up and to pull
down, and to waste and to destroy, and to build and to plant,"
was made concerning the Church and Ecclesiastical power. For
Mr. Gladstone says :[5] " Up to 1870, opinion in the Roman
Church on all matters involving civil liberty . . . . was
free whenever it was resolute." Nevertheless, he is conscious
that the decrees of 1870 did not alter the question in debate ; for
he says :[6] " The theory which placed every human being, in
things spiritual and things temporal, at the feet of the Roman
Pontiff, had not been an *idolum specûs*, a mere theory of the
chamber. Brain power, never surpassed in the political history
of the world, had been devoted for centuries to the single purpose

---

[1] p. 10.   [2] p. 10.   [3] p. 11.   [4] p. 11.   [5] p. 57.   [6] p. 27.

of working it into the practice of Christendom. . . . What was really material, therefore, was, not whether the Papal Chair laid claim to this or that particular power, but whether it laid claim to some power that included them all, and whether that claim had received such sanction from the authorities of the Latin Church, that there remained within her borders absolutely no tenable standing ground from which war against it could be maintained. Did the Pope then claim infallibility? or did he . . . . claim an universal obedience from his flock?" He at once answers his own question[1]: "The Popes had kept up with comparatively little intermission, for well-nigh a thousand years, their claim to dogmatic infallibility; and had, at periods within the same tract of time, often enough made, and never retracted, that other claim, which is theoretically less, but practically larger,—their claim to an obedience, virtually universal, from the baptised members of the Church." It follows that the decrees of 1870 made no *practical* difference in the point at issue.

Yet, under the fallacious assumption that the decrees of the Vatican have made some *practical* difference in the supremacy or indirect power of the Pontiff, Mr. Gladstone repeats, in various forms, the issue which he has brought into controversy. For example[2]—"The Pope's infallibility, when he speaks *ex cathedrâ* on faith and morals, has been declared, with the assent of the bishops of the Roman Church, to be an article of faith, binding on the conscience of every Christian; his claim to the obedience of his spiritual subjects has been declared, in like manner, with ut any practical limit or reserve; and his supremacy, without any reserve of civil rights, has been similarly affirmed to include everything which relates to the discipline and government of the Church throughout the world." Mr. Gladstone then argues that infallibility in faith and morals includes every department and

---

[1] p. 28.   [2] p. 32.

function of life; and that the supreme direction of us, in respect
of every duty, then necessarily belongs to the head of the Church.
Moreover, he asserts that, even outside the sphere of infallibility,
the Pontiff claims an absolute and entire obedience, so that even
where his judgments are not infallible, they are yet "unappealable
and irreversible, and no person may pass judgment upon them,
and all men . . . . . are bound truly to obey them."[1]

This assertion, we may remark in passing, is founded on two
imperfect quotations from the dogmatic constitutions. If Mr.
Gladstone had consulted the originals for himself, he would not
have quoted merely parts of sentences, omitting clauses at the
beginning.[2] The entire sentences are as follows (the omitted
words being in italics) : *" Hence we teach and declare that, by the
appointment of our Lord, the Roman Church possesses a superiority
of ordinary power over all other Churches, and that this power of
jurisdiction of the Roman Pontiff, which is truly episcopal, is
immediate; to which all,* of whatever rite and dignity, both
pastors and faithful, both individually and collectively are bound,
by their duty of hierarchical subordination and true obedience,
to submit, not only in matters which belong to faith and morals,
but also in those that appertain to the discipline and government
of the Church throughout the world, *so that the Church of Christ
may be one flock under one Supreme Pastor through the preservation
of unity both of communion, and of profession of the same faith
with the Roman Pontiff.* This is the teaching of Catholic truth,
from which no one can deviate without loss of faith and of
salvation." *" And since, by the Divine Right of Apostolic primacy,
the Roman Pontiff is placed over the Universal Church,* we further
teach and declare that he is the Supreme Judge of the faithful,
and that, in all causes, the decision of which belongs to the
Church, recourse may be had to this tribunal, and that none may
re-open the judgment of the Apostolic See, the authority of

---

[1] p. 38.   [2] p.

which is greater than all other, nor can any lawfully review its judgment." This latter one, we may remind the reader, is entirely made up of quotations (1), from the Brief, "*super soliditate*," of Pius VI. (Nov. 28, 1786); (2), from the Acts of the xivth Œcumenical Council the 2nd of Lyons (1274); and (3), from an epistle of Pope Nicholas I., "*ad Michælem Imp.*" (A.D. 858); so that it is a mistake to charge the Church with this Doctrine, as an example of "a policy of violence and change," inaugurated by the present Pontiff in 1870.

But to conclude the rehearsal of the various forms in which Mr. Gladstone states the question at issue : he says [1] that the Pontiff is not content to deal thus with individuals alone, but that "The State also must be a slave." [2] He then takes up the position that such principles are repugnant to civil allegiance. There we join issue with him. That, therefore, is the *status quæstionis*.

The proofs adduced in support of this position are very fragile. What are they? "It is notorious," says he, without adducing a single example, or giving us a single reference,—"it is notorious," he says, that the infliction of penalty in life, limb, liberty, or goods, on disobedient members of the Christian Church, and the title to depose sovereigns, and to release subjects from their allegiance, with all its revolting consequences, have been "declared and decreed by Rome, that is to say, by Popes and Papal Councils; and the stringent condemnations of the Syllabus include all those who hold that Popes and Papal Councils have transgressed the just limits of their power, or usurped the rights of princes." Now, the Pontiff is the head of a perfect Society, and therefore must have a full power, legislative, judicial, and executive or coercitive. Popes and their Councils have, in virtue of that power and authority, punished refractory criminals, and pronounced sentence of deposition

---

[1] p. 39.   [2] p. 40.

against wicked and tyrannical sovereigns who refused to amend
and observe the laws of God in their dealings with their subjects
and with other States ; but, I assert, and am prepared presently
to show that, in doing this, they did not transgress the limits of
their own power, nor usurp the rights of princes. Does this
concession, full and unreserved as it is, suffice to prove that I do
not bear allegiance to my sovereign, Queen Victoria ? I deny it.
I yield to no man in loyalty and faithfulness to the Queen.

Mr. Gladstone acknowledges that there is a law above us,
above the State, above the Queen herself ; yes, the same eternal law
above all the emperors and kings of the earth ; above the Supreme
Pontiff himself. Mr. Gladstone thus expresses himself in speaking
of the limits of jurisdiction of the Sovereign ; he makes this
concession : [1] "There are millions upon millions of the Protestants
of this country who would agree with Archbishop Manning if he
were simply telling us that Divine truth is not to be sought from
the lips of the State, nor to be sacrificed at its command." There
is, then, truth or a law over all the earth ? Let me ask him,
where is the organ of that law ? Where is the judge which is to
interpret, and the executive power to enforce that law ? If a
king were to command a subject to do an unrighteous act,
would a loyal subject obey ? If a John suggests the murder of
Prince Arthur, is a faithful Hubert to fulfil the behest, and
perform the deed of darkness ? Let Mr. Gladstone remember
St. Maurice and the Theban Legion, and answer this question : Is
there not verily a law superior to sovereigns, and states, and
parliaments which emperors, and kings, and representative
assemblies must obey ? Who, then, is the visible Ruler who is
to declare that law and put it in force, and secure justice and
right dealing on the whole earth ? 'The Church,' he is sure to
answer; 'the Church was instituted by our Lord for this purpose,
as I have fully shown in my two books on 'Church and State,'

---

[1] p. 55.

and in numerous speeches and publications since.' Yes; but the Church on earth—the Church Militant—is an organization of human beings; the law must be declared for them; their doubts must be resolved, their controversies ended. That, even, is not enough; there must be a Living Authority among men, a Living Authority at the head of that Church Militant to carry out the law. How can that be done without respect, obedience, submission on the part of all the subjects of that Authority—all the members of that Church Militant? Here I am; I stand before him, and I ask him to answer me honestly and sincerely, as man to man,—and I am one of the many who do believe in Mr. Gladstone's sincerity and honesty,—I ask him to answer my question; I challenge him to give a reply. Surely he will not tell me that St. Maurice was a devil? Let him read, I pray, the "*Mirari vos.*"

He may, indeed, go off at a tangent; very likely! He may turn round upon me and repeat his words about the Pontiff being autocratic, and absolute, and gifted with unlimited power, while all other men and states must be infinitely slavish in their submission. What? has he not read the answer which Count Joseph de Maistre gave to that very question: What is there to restrain the Pope? "Everything—canons, laws, national customs, monarchs, tribunals, national assemblies, prescription, remonstrances, negociations, duty, fear, prudence, and especially public opinion, the queen of the world." These restrain him in those questions where the law of God (or the Canon law, which is merely the application in detail of the laws of God) do not mark out his course. Or, as Mr. Gladstone seems to have a tenderness for Dr. Döllinger, let him consult his "Church and the Churches," at p. 46, and then turn to the words of Pope Pius VII. at p. 48.[1]

Now, perhaps, he will agree with me that the Pontiff is not

---

[1] I have not the book by me, but I believe these references are correct.

"autocratic," and that the claim to obedience advanced in the third chapter of the Vatican constitutions, is not the claim of a despot.

Let us return to Mr. Gladstone's Third Proposition again : how does he attempt to prove "That no one can become a convert to the Roman Catholic Church, without renouncing his moral and mental freedom, and placing his civil loyalty and duty at the mercy of another ? "[1] Until this century, he says in proof, every human being lay bound, in spiritual and temporal (*i.e.*, in *all*) things, at the feet of the Roman Pontiff. But in 1816-17 a select Committee of the House of Commons collected evidence to show that "the doctrines of deposition and universal dominion were obsolete beyond revival ; " even[2] "the Council of Constance had, in act as well as word, shown that the Pope's judgments, and the Pope himself, were triable by the assembled representatives of the Christian world." Surely Mr. Gladstone knew that this part of the Acts of the Council of Constance is wholly without weight or authority ; it was not confirmed by the Holy See, and therefore was not an expression of the mind of the Church. That part is neither here nor there. The Acts of the 4th and 5th Sessions of Constance, which declare the superiority of a Council to the Pope, are of no authority. The Council had not at that time been convoked ; it was therefore not a Council, but only an Assembly, a gathering, a caucus. Afterwards Gregory XII. did convene the Council ; and then it was a true Council, and its Acts were confirmed : that is to say, such of the Acts as had been passed " conciliariter," were confirmed by Pope Martin V., and became valid. With regard to the subject matter,—the subordination of the Pope to a Council,—it may be as well to remark that the authority or power of Bishops united, is no greater than that of each Bishop alone. St. Cyprian, for example, declares that every Bishop holds the Episcopate *in solido*.

---

[1] p. 12. [2] p. 29.

But the Apostolate is not included in the Episcopate; nor is it created by the Episcopate, nor even developed from the Episcopate. In the Episcopate, the Bishop of Rome is only the equal of every other Bishop; but he is the superior of all Bishops by the Apostolate. The Apostolate is attached to the Roman See; which is, therefore, called the Apostolic See, and "the Mother and Mistress of all the Churches." The Apostolate descended from St. Peter to his successors in the See of Rome. It is a distinct power or authority which was given to St. Peter. It is not the same as the Episcopate, which every Bishop possesses. It includes the Episcopate, while the Episcopate does not include the Apostolate. The Pope holds the Apostolic authority direct from God; while every Bishop holds the Episcopal authority, or jurisdiction, by delegation from the Pope; although he received the Episcopal character, in consecration, from God. Herein lies the question of investitures.

To continue Mr. Gladstone's argument in support of his Third Proposition: The Council of Trent, he says, "neither affirmed nor denied" anything relating to the subject.[1] A Committee of the House of Lords collected evidence in 1825, when Bishop Doyle is reported to have given the following evidence [I have not the report by me for verification; but I accept Mr. Gladstone's statement, as he has probably verified it for himself] :—

> Q. "In what, and how far does the Roman Catholic profess to obey the Pope?"
>
> A. "The Catholic professes to obey the Pope in matters which regard his religious faith, and in those matters of ecclesiastical disipline *which have already been defined* by the competent authorities."
>
> Q. "Does that justify the objection that is made to Catholics, that their allegiance is divided?"

---

[1] p. 29.

A. " I do not think it does in any way ; we are bound to obey the Pope in those things that I have already mentioned ; but our obedience to the law, and the allegiance which we owe the Sovereign, are complete and full, and perfect, and undivided, *inasmuch as they extend to all political, legal, and civil rights of the king or of his subjects.* I think the allegiance due to the King, and the allegiance due to the Pope, are as *distinct,* and as divided in their nature, as any two things can possibly be."

That is quite true ; they are distinct ; but they are not conflicting, for they are subalternate. We do owe a full, perfect, and undivided allegiance to our Sovereign in regard to all political, legal, and civil rights of the Sovereign or subjects ; but not in regard to matters outside this order, and beyond the King's sphere. Dr. Doyle probably added that although he owed full allegiance to the King, yet that he was bound " to obey God rather than men ;" and in saying so, he would not have been contradicting himself. Dr. Doyle's words do not, therefore, prove that which Mr. Gladstone has quoted them in order to substantiate.

To proceed with Mr. Gladstone's supposed proof. The Vicars Apostolic of Great Britain published, in 1826, a declaration to the same effect as that of Dr Doyle ; and the Hierarchy of Ireland, in the same year, issued a pastoral containing these words :[1] " They declare, on oath, their belief *that it is not an article of the Catholic Faith,* neither are they thereby *required* to believe that the Pope is infallible." This was perfectly true ; for as it had not, at that time, been defined, it was not an article of faith. Yet it is probable—I feel sure—that they all did freely believe it, although not one of them was *required* to believe it.

In fine, the Commission on the Maynooth College (says

---

[1] p. 31.

Mr. Gladstone), reported in 1855 : " We see no reason to believe that there has been any disloyalty in the teaching of the College, or any disposition to impair the obligations of an unreserved allegiance to your Majesty."[1]

' Yes,' says Mr. Gladstone, ' that is very true; but here is my point in the argument in support of my Third Proposition : Since that time, namely in 1870, the dogma of the Infallibility has been declared to be an article of the faith of the Church,— declared by the whole Church, assembled at Rome, in the legal representatives of every part of the Church.' Well, that does not impair our allegiance, as I will presently show. Let us first, however, hear the rest of Mr. Gladstone's argument. He next avers that this dogma was not, in 1870, declared by the Church to be an article of the Faith, because the declaration was informal,— informal because the canons are not in the same form as those of the Council of Trent, but begin " Pius Episcopus, &c., &c." A Saturday Reviewer (Nov. 14th) has incautiously followed Mr. Gladstone, as if the argument had some weight. Let me tell them, however, that every Bull, and every Constitution, and every Act of a Council requires the Pope's confirmation, if the Pope is not present in the Council; and it cannot be promulgated until the Pope has formally confirmed it. But, whenever the Pope is present in council, the form is always such as that of the Vatican decree; for the Pope promulgates it in the council, and it wants no further confirmation. Surely Mr. Gladstone, a Privy Councillor, knows the difference between " an Order of the Privy Council" and an " Order in Council," the Queen being present when the latter is made. Yet Mr. Gladstone imagines that the Vatican decrees have, therefore, not the authority of the Church, although every Bishop signed his name to this declaration : " *Ego, judicans, sic definio.*"

Mr. Gladstone also takes a further exception to the decree of

---

Infallibility, on the ground that the term *ex cathedrâ* has not been defined. Yet it is defined in the very passage which Mr. Gladstone has quoted :[1] "*Id est cum, omnium Christianorum Pastoris et Doctoris munere fungens.*" That is, when the Pope formally promulgates a doctrine, as the Head and Organ of the Church, appending some words to indicate that it is an official act. I may also remind Mr. Gladstone that the concluding words of his quotation : "Ideoque *ejusmodi* Romani Pontificis definitiones ex sese, non autem ex consensu Ecclesiæ, irreformabiles esse," are the words of Pope Nicholas I., in the 9th century; used afterwards in 1085 by the synod of Quedlinburgh.

Let us pause for a moment, to remark that, if the definition is not binding, Mr. Gladstone's argument is suicidal; for then all things have remained as they were before. If, on the other hand, it is binding, then certainly his argument does not suffice to prove his Third Proposition : that we have resigned our moral and mental freedom and abjured our allegiance. For no one resigns his moral freedom by knowing certainly what is right, nor his mental freedom in knowing with certainty what is true; and in this case the Church has declared what is right and true. As to allegiance, I will presently enlarge upon that point.

Mr. Gladstone affirms, however, that, until 1870, the two jurisdictions (of Sovereign and of the Supreme Pontiff) were separate—(he doubtless means "distinct;" they were never separate, as they were always subalternate). Yet he says[2] that this was undone by the Syllabus and Encyclical in 1864, and by the Vatican Council in 1870. Mr. Gladstone's mind here labours under a serious confusion, as we shall presently see. The two jurisdictions have always been held to be distinct and subalternate,—the temporal sword being under the spiritual sword. Neither the Encyclical, nor the Syllabus, nor the Vatican

---

[1] p. 34.   [2] p. 40.

Council, nor any Bull, nor Brief, nor decree, has in the least changed this.

We shall soon revert to this point. We must first notice a curious little addition to Mr. Gladstone's argument :[1] " Even in the United States, where the severance between Church and State is supposed to be complete, a long catalogue might be drawn of subjects belonging to the domain and competency of the State, but also undeniably affecting the Government of the Church. . . .(After enumerating these subjects, he continues)— In Europe the circle is far wider, the points of contact and of interlacing almost innumerable." The word " Church " does not here, of course, denote the Roman Catholic Church. What Mr. Gladstone means is : that there is, in the United States, no Established Church, and that even there we find a conflict of jurisdiction, while in Europe, where there are Established Churches, the evil is much greater, and the conflict exacerbated. What is the only conclusion which can legitimately be drawn ? Ergo, disestablish the Church of England as fast as you can ! But what has this to say to that which had to be proved, namely, his Third Proposition ?

There is yet another question on this point which we must beg Mr. Gladstone to answer. Does he mean that in all these subjects the Holy See wrongfully claims the obedience of its members, while they ought to yield implicit and unreasoning obedience therein to the State ? If not, his position is untenable. Pass your eye over the subjects mentioned. " Marriage :" Will Mr. Gladstone obey the State if it commands a purely civil marriage ? " Burial :" Would Mr. Gladstone obey the State in a matter of cremation, sending his friends to the fire, when perhaps, with patience, it may be done better than the State can do it ? "Education:" Yes, he may go in for a mere secular education, at the order of the State. " Blasphemy :" If the

---

[1] p. 41.

State orders him to do so, he will obey! But I need not prolong the catalogue. Mr. Gladstone cuts me short, and says impatiently : ' No, therein I would not obey the State; my conscience will not permit.' Then the State has no right to your obedience ? It may not determine in what cases it may demand your obedience ? The State may not fix the limits of its own jurisdiction ! Ergo, *cadet quæstio.* So frail and utterly irrelevant is the argument on which Mr. Gladstone's whole case is made to rest !

Before passing to our (the Catholic) view of the matter, I must notice one slip (if I rightly interpret the very involved and Gladstonian sentence) :[1] " There have always been, and there still are (*sic*) no small proportion of our race, and those by no means in all respects the worst, who are sorely open to the temptation, especially in times of religious disturbance, to discharge their spiritual responsibilities by *power of attorney* ;[2] as advertising houses find custom in proportion, not so much to the solidity of their resources as to the magniloquence of their premises (*sic*) and assurances, so, theological boldness in the extension of such claims is sure to pay (*sic*), by widening certain circles of devoted adherents, however, it may repel the mass of mankind." I suppose he means by this sentence, that there is a tendency in some persons to let others think and act for them : confiding persons, without guile or suspicion ; or else, persons who have a strong sense of their own short-comings and want of knowledge. Now, a power of attorney is all very well, if the attorney is properly qualified. I have no doubt that Mr. Gladstone lets an attorney act for him in any legal business which may arise; and he asks a doctor to think for him when he is sick. Yet Mr. Gladstone would surely not tell me that his attorney is a perfect lawyer, whose judgment, on any case, would be decisive ; nor would he assert that his doctor is a perfect and infallible healer of all sickness. How much more foolish of Mr. Gladstone, then,

---

[1] p. 46. [2] The italics are Mr. Gladstone's own.

to act thus, than it is in the "no small proportion of our race" to trust to an "Attorney" who is properly and perfectly qualified. But let us put aside Mr. Gladstone's simile: the "attorney" means the Head of the Church, and the "theological boldness" means the definition of Infallibility. I will now ask Mr. Gladstone how he thinks that these promises of our Lord have been fulfilled—"Whatsoever ye shall bind on earth, shall be bound in heaven," &c.; and, "Lo, I am with you always, even unto the end of the world;" and, "I will give you the Spirit of truth, who shall lead you unto all truth." These promises were consequent on a command—"Go, and teach all nations." The powers were promised for the fulfilment of the command. So much for the "attorney." Now for the "no small proportion of our race:" Has he pondered on the meaning of this: "Except you become as a little child you cannot enter the kingdom of heaven"? The characteristic of a child is a humble confidingness and trust. A child learns by taking on trust what his parents and tutors may say; and he acts as his superiors direct him. Is that the character of the Protestant or of the Catholic?

Before passing to our side of the question, I must be allowed to notice what I think to be errors on p. 58. The first is the assertion that "The Constitutions of Clarendon,—the work of the English Bishops" were "cursed from the Papal throne." Mr. Gladstone has not vouchsafed to give us any references in support either of this statement or of the other on the same page; and I am unable to find any such assertion in any work which I possess here in my dwelling by the "melancholy Ocean" and plangent wave. But I have found assertions which warrant me in contradicting both this statement and the other. Let us take the latest historical works: "The Constitutional History of England," by Professor Stubbs, printed at the Clarendon Press of the University of Oxford, in 1874; and the "Select Charters," by the same learned author, and printed at the same time and place. This is the account given at p. 464 of the former work:

"After two or three unsatisfactory interviews with Becket, the king called together at Clarendon, in January, 1164, the whole body of the bishops and barons. Again the archbishop was bidden to accept the customs in use under Henry I.; and again he declined doing anything unconditionally. Then the king ordered that they should be reduced to writing, having been first ascertained by recognition. The recognitors, according to the formal record, were the archbishops, bishops, earls, barons, and most noble and ancient men of the kingdom; according to the archbishop, Richard de Lucy, the justiciar, and Jocelin de Bailleul, a French lawyer, of whom little else is known, were the real authors of the document, which was presented as the result of the inquiry, and which has become famous under the name of the 'Constitutions of Clarendon.' The 'Constitutions of Clarendon' are sixteen in number, and purport to be, as may be inferred from their production, a codification of the usages of Henry I. on the disputed points. They concern questions of advowson and presentation, churches in the King's gift, the trials of clerks, the security to be taken of the excommunicated, the trials of laymen for spiritual offences, the excommunication of tenants-in-chief, the licence of the clergy to go abroad, ecclesiastical appeals which are not to go further than the archbishop without the consent of the King, questions of the title to ecclesiastical estates, the baronial duties of the prelates, the election to bishoprics and abbacies, the right of the King to the goods of felons deposited under the protection of the Church, and the ordination of villains."

At p. 135 of the latter work ('Charters') we find the obnoxious articles—in the sense in which Mr. Gladstone would perhaps have framed them—against the Papal authority, and in favour of Ecclesiastical usurpations by the civil power. Such as "the reservation to the Curia Regis of questions of Presentation and Advowson;" "the maintenance of the distinction [i.e., limits] of the ecclesiastical and civil jurisdictions which had been introduced into England by William the Conqueror," and prevention of appeals to Rome; "the direction that elections to bishopricks and abbacies shall take place in the Chapel Royal, subject to the approval of the King and his Council;" "the restriction of the liberty of 'rustics' or 'natives' to take holy orders," in order that the landowners might not lose the services of their labourers, &c., &c. Here, then, we have the marks of strife against the Church; but we do not find that the Supreme Pontiff *cursed* them; although he, no doubt, disapproved of them, as did the Archbishop of Canterbury. Nay, we do find, according to Professor Anstey, that "The obnoxious clauses in the Constitutions of Clarendon were revoked by the Monarch, with the assent of his Curia (Privy Council); and peace was restored to the Commonwealth by maintaining its laws."

The other assertion is that the Archbishop, "Stephen Langton, headed the barons of England in extorting from the Papal minion John, ... that Magna Charta (of 1215) which the Pope at once visited with his anathemas." Here is another battle-field in the same campaign of centuries,—the war of the Church against the world. Turning to p. 339 of Professor Stubbs's "charters," we find the words : "It is curious to mark the Papal sanction given by Gualo to the Charter (of Henry III. in 1216), the original enactment of which had subjected *the barons* to the sentence of excommunication." The barons were excommunicated; we do not read that the Charter was "anathematized!" Why had the Barons been excommunicated? Because they did not evince allegiance to their sovereign, but had risen in revolt! Just so other Popes, as I have mentioned in my lecture on "Civilisation and the See of Rome," had anathematized other subjects for rising in revolt. On turning to the account of John's Charter in 1215,[1] we read : "On the 27th of April, the day fixed for the king's answer, the barons assembled in force at Brackley. The king, who was

---

[1] Stubbs, p. 290.

at Oxford, sent to ask the details of their claims; and, whilst refusing to grant them, proposed (May 10) an arbitration to be made by the Pope and eight persons,—four to be chosen by himself, and four by the barons.   But before this was done they had (May 5), at Reading or at Wallingford, renounced their allegiance to John, and begun to attack the Royal Castle." Further, Professor Stubbs gives, at length,[1] the " Sentence of excommunication *against trans-gressors of the Charters."* The character of this whole struggle is given by Professor Anstey, in his " Lectures on the Laws and Constitutions of England."[2]   The distinction of Powers was no longer in question.   It became a struggle, upon whose issue depended, not the maintenance of both as of two co-ordinate authorities, but the predominance of the one, and that the least intelligent. . . . Had she (the Church) succumbed in the contest, she must inevitably have ended by becoming that *Thing,* which the Greek Church had already submitted to become, the merest engine of temporal administration.   To her, therefore, the struggle was one of life and death.[3]   But here *was* resistance, and the Church was saved."

These arguments, therefore, drawn by Mr. Gladstone from the same struggle in former days, seem entirely fallacious.

Mr. Gladstone, having, as he imagines, proved his position, (that the principles of the Catholic Church are contradictory to a subject's loyalty towards his temporal sovereign) proceeds to draw his conclusion. What is it? That the people of this country[4] have to expect from Catholics " some declaration or manifestation of opinion " against " the ecclesiastical party " who promulgated those principles.   He demands that we shall[5] "sweep away. . . . the presumptive imputations which our ecclesiastical rulers at Rome, acting autocratically, appear to have brought upon our capacity to pay a solid and undivided allegiance."   In order to

---

[1] p. 373.   [2] p. 148.
[3] Eichhorn's Deutsche Staats-und-Rechts Geschichte.   Part II. § 276-9.
[4] p. 7.   [5] p. 43.

this, there is required [1] " either a demonstration that neither in the name of faith, nor in the name of morals, nor in the name of the government or discipline of the Church, is the Pope of Rome able . . . . to make any claim upon those who adhere to his communion, of such a nature as can impair the integrity of their civil allegiance ; or else that, if and when such claim is made, it will . . . . be repelled and rejected."

Shall we tell Mr. Gladstone that, if he had not been beguiled by his prompter into dealing unfairly with us Catholics, he would have found sufficient for this purpose in that Syllabus which he thought to quote against us—For example, the condemnation of the proposition : " It is lawful to refuse obedience to legitimate princes and even to rebel against them ;"[2] or,[3] the condemnation of the proposition : " Authority is nothing else but numerical power and material force ;"—or in the Acts of the Council of Constance (of which he has endeavoured to make use), which enforce submission to rulers; or in the Brief of Pope Gregory XVI. against Lammenais; or in the Encyclical " Qui pluribus," November 9th, 1846 ; or in the Allocution " Quisque Vestrûm," October 4th, 1847 ; or in the Encyclical " Nostis et Vobiscum," December 8th, 1849 ; or in the Apostolic Letter " Cum Catholicâ," March 26th, 1860 ; or in numbers of other authoritative documents. The Brief " Mirari Vos " against Lammenais, contains this sentence among many others : " Præclara hæc immobilis subjectionis in principes exempla, quæ ex sanctissimis christianæ religionis præceptis necessariò proficiscebantur, detestandam illorum insolentiam et improbitatem condemnant, qui projectâ effrenatâque procacis libertatis cupiditate æstuantes, toti in eo sunt, qui jura quæque principatuum labefactent at que convellant, &c."

Yet, Mr. Gladstone says:[4] that " England is entitled to ask and to know in what way the obedience required by the Pope and the Council of the Vatican is to be reconciled with the integrity

---

[1] p. 44.　　　[2] Prop lxiii., xiii. or [3]Prop. lx., x.　　　[4] p. 43.

of civil allegiance." Now, I will not repeat what I have said already, that Catholics always believed in the infallibility of the Church; but will endeavour to tell him in what way obedience to the Pope is reconciled with civil allegiance. If I were to answer in one word, I would follow the example of S. Dionysius, and say : By subordination. But I will enter into this at length.

Wherever society has been fully organised, we observe, in the whole society, a Heirarchy of Societies (if I may so employ the term),—a Heirarchy of Societies one within the other, and one subordinate to the other. There is first the family ; ruled by its natural head, who is supreme within his sphere. This monarchical government is absolute, so long as natural Justice, Divine Law, State Law, Municipal Law, and Parish Law are not infringed. Secondly, there is the Parish (or Commune), which is made up of families. This Republic consists of the heads of families in Vestry (or Village Parliament) assembled, and is supreme in all that concerns it alone. But it may not step out of its sphere, nor infringe the Laws of God, nor the laws of the Superior Societies. Thirdly, we have the Municipal Government in towns, and County Government in rural districts. These are made up of Parishes (or wards), and manage their own affairs, and cannot be interfered with by the State so long as they do not travel out of their own sphere and transgress their proper limits; and so long, of course, as they do not violate the law of Justice. Their Government is aristocratic, consisting, as it does, of chosen men (picked men, or the best men, ἄριστοι). Over the municipalities and counties there used to be the Province, which was ruled by a Governor, or Lord Lieutenant, with his council, and with the advice of his parliament; (such as each of our Colonies at present, and the Isle of Man, and the Channel Islands). The Province was, in fact, the image of the State, and was supreme so long as it touched only its own affairs, and did not transgress its limits. Then there was the State, which was made up of Provinces. It also was supreme in its own sphere, and managed, without interference, its own affairs. But it, too, must not travel out of its province, nor break the law, natural and divine, which is above it. In Germany there used, moreover, to be, above the State, an Empire, which was made up of Sovereign States, federated together under one Head, with his council and advising parliament.

Here was a subalternation of authorities, to each of which every man owed allegiance; and his loyalty and obedience to the one was, by the principle of subordination, perfectly "reconciled" with his loyalty and obedience to another. Lastly, at the top of the Hierarchy of Societies, was the Holy Church, which federated all christian states in one. It is the most perfect society, and rests upon a Divine Foundation. It is a Theocracy,—the Head being appointed by God to be the Expositor, Interpreter, and Enforcer of the Law of God throughout the Christian World.

The parish, the municipality and county, and the province, are creations of man, and are at the will of the State. The family, the State, and the Church are not created by the will of man (for God has told us that He has set bounds to the nations); and the family springs from a union which God has made: "Whom God hath joined." The two former are natural societies; but the Church is the supernatural society. Hence the triple Crown of the Supreme Pontiff: the Paternal, the Royal, and the Pontifical Crown. For he is the Universal Father, a Sovereign, and the Vicar of Christ over the Universal Church.

"Omnis potestas a Deo est; et quæ sunt, a Deo ordinata sunt." That is, every society has its proper ruler, and all are subalternate, or *ordered;* the lower being in subordination to the higher. There are two modes in which a thing may be subordinate; either as a species to its genus, or as a proximate end (means) is related to its final cause or ultimate end. In both ways societies are subordinate; but here it is necessary only to consider the latter. Societies are subalternate, because their proper ends are subalternate; and the end of a lower one is a means to the end of a higher; and the end of the highest is the ultimate end of all, and of every individual. As St. Thomas of Aquin wrote: [De Reg. Princ. I. xiv.] "Opportet eundem finem esse multitudinis humanæ, qui est hominis unius. Non est ergo ultimus finis multitudinis congregatæ vivere secundum virtutem; sed per virtuosam vitam pervenire ad fruitionem divinam." As, then, the proximate end (any mean) is in subordination to every higher end, so is every State in subordination to the Church. This does not, however, interfere with the autonomy of each State; because each kind of society and each society is independent within its own sphere. But as each superior society has to keep each of its subordinate societies from transgressing its own sphere, so it is the duty of the Church to restrain every State from stepping out of its province and violating its limits;—or, in other words, She must prevent it from breaking the laws and the order established by God.

Thus it is that society is an organism. An organism; consisting of many elements or parts, also organised, and having a corporate life of its own. Society is not an unformed mass or multitude, dead, inert, chaotic. So S. Dionysius says (as quoted by Pope Boniface VIII. and the Roman Council in the "*Unam Sanctam*,") " The law of God's order is, that the lowest things are reduced to order (subordinated), by intermediate things, to the highest. Therefore, according to the law of the Universe, all things are not reduced to order in an equality and immediately; but the lowest things are reduced to order by intermediate things (means), and those lower things by the highest." S. Augustine, also, compares a perfect society to a musical harmony, which consists in a proper proportion and subordination of the phrases and chords and individual sounds, to each other, and to the whole; and as the effect of this proportion is to produce in the audience a sense of pleasure, so, in the civil society, peace, common wellbeing, and the highest civil happiness, come from the right and just proportion or subordination of the different members of that one body,—the society,—towards each other, and towards the whole body. S. Thomas Aquinatis takes his conception of society from a living organism, or human body, with its informing soul· It is all moved by one living principle, to which each member is in subordination, each having its proper function and activity, which it exercises for itself, but which redounds to the common good.[1] To come down from great to small, or from the middle ages to the xix.th century, I will quote M. Bastiat's *Harmonies Economiques*: "Dieu n'a pas déployé dans le mécanisme social, moins de bonté touchante, d'admirable simplicité, de magnifique splendeur, que dans la mécanique céleste."

Here, then, we are at serious issue with Liberalism, and its organ and exponent, Mr. Gladstone. Liberalism says that the provinces of rulers are not distinct, but separate ; not subalternate, but contradictory. In short, Liberalism avers that society is not an organism with a corporate life ; but a confused chaotic mass, or plum-pudding, in which nothing has its place, and in which no order dwells. The spheres of rulers are separate and contradictory (think Mr. Gladstone and Liberalism), and, therefore, a man must belong either to one ruler or to the other. Of course, if the two positions are contradictory ; but of course not, if they are subalternate. The assertion that the provinces are contradictory, was the condemned error of Abellard and of his pupil Arnoldo da Brescia, the Republican and Revolutionist. Condemned by " a true Council," shall we say ? Yet Mr. Gladstone says of every Catholic, " he must owe allegiance either to the Queen or to the Pope ; he cannot be a Catholic with the Pope and loyal to the Queen." Is not that the issue put before us in his pamphlet ? is not that his grand charge, accusation and indictment which he has laid against us ? Therefore, he thinks that the rule of the Queen and the rule of the Pope are mutually excluding or contradictory ;—repugnant, at least. In reply, we say: No ! a thousand times, No ! We owe the strictest

---

[1] See his De Regimine Principum, I. 12 and IV. 23.

allegiance to the Queen, and yield to no subject of her realms in loyalty (for it is a sentiment with them, while for us loyalty is a religious duty); we also owe the same to the Pope; because the one power is subordinate to the other, just as the end of the State is subordinate to the end of the Church, and as the body is subordinate to the soul.

All the various kinds of societies, which I have mentioned, are of different natures, with diverse origins and diverse ends; but yet they are composed of the same persons, or subjects; that is to say, every person is under various jurisdictions, is moved by various powers, and is directed by various ordinating and guiding principles. Different sets of obligations are inherent in the same person; because the ends of the societies are different. Yet there is no contradiction of jurisdiction, no confusion of duties, no conflicting of obligations, because they are subalternate—the lower being subordinate to the higher. How can a man-of-war be under the command of many officers unless one officer is subordinate to another officer? Yet it is a common saying at sea, that "there are more captains than ropes." How, again, can a patient be under two doctors, if those two doctors act separately? The doctors are distinct persons; but one must be subordinate to the other, or woe betides the poor patient. So it is throughout the order of God in the universe; and only so can we say: "Sic transeamus per bona temporalia, ut non amittamus æterna."[1]

One great prerogative example—as Lord Bacon would say— one great representative example of this principle of subordination has been for centuries the battle-field of parties—Guelph and Ghibelline, Tory and Whig, and what not. I mean the two great divisions of society—temporal and spiritual. The ends of all civil societies are temporal ends; the end of the spiritual society, or Church, is eternal. The subjects of both are the same men; only the main ends are different. For man is both body and spirit,

---

[1] Roman Missal.

which are distinct, but not separate. When they are separate the man is dead. Yet man is an indivisible personality; because the body is subordinate to the spirit. So it is that every man is ordered to two main ends, which are not contradictory because subalternate; and thus the civil society, which has the care of one end, is subordinate to the society which looks after the other end. The one end is fulfilled on this earth (temporal happiness); the other is only begun on this earth : " Habetis fructum vestrum in sanctificationem; finem verò, vitam æternam." (Rom. vi. 22.) So S. Thomas the Christian philosopher of Aquin says, that the necessities of the temporal kingdom—all that belongs to the conservation of the social, municipal, family, and individual life— the king must take especial care to provide. Yet the necessities of the Christian commonwealth, and Spiritual life, are by far more important. Therefore, he says, the former are subordinate to the latter. In other words : The life with which the State is cognizant, and which is the end of the State, is only a means towards gaining the eternal life. But the powers, which direct to the ends, must stand in the same order as the ends themselves; and so the State is subordinate to the Church.

By the nature of things, whenever we are considering any matter which belongs exclusively to either Church or State, no dispute or question of jurisdiction can arise. Those disputes surge up in regard to matters which each of them may claim as within its own sphere. For example : The State may, by conscription, order all men to serve in the army. The Church then says that Priests must be exempt, that they may devote themselves to the salvation of souls. Or, The Church proclaims certain holydays of obligation. The State then says that, unless men work on those days, the amount of production will be reduced. Now, which is to have the hegemony ? Either the Pope must have, with a *direct* authority over exclusively religious matters, an *indirect* power over civil matters; or else kings must have a *direct* authority over political matters, as well as an *indirect* authority over religious questions. Of these two things, one. There is no third case possible. In other words, kings must be subordinate to the Sovereign Pontiff, or else the Pontiff must be the subject of some one king.

Let us pause, and turn aside for a moment, and sit down by the way-side, while we ponder over that term " indirect" power or authority. Indirect power is the same as that which is sometimes called directive power, or *potestas directiva*. For the word " direct," one day, got up and turned its back upon itself. Its meaning has circumgyrated. We must then distinguish between the direct power of a ruler in his own sphere, and the indirect, or directive, power of his superior in the same sphere. Suarez, for example, makes this distinction.[1] " Directa vocatur (potestas) quæ est intra finem et terminos ejusdem potestatis; indirecta, quæ solum nascitur ex directione ad finem altiorem et ad superiorem ac excellentiorem potestatem pertinentem." So the State orders matters towards a merely temporal end,—namely, the greatest happiness of the society in the present life ; and that is why it is called temporal power, or civil power. In the temporal or civil order or sphere, this authority is of course supreme ; that is, where the ultimate termination of any resolution is in that sphere. But civil or temporal happiness has to be referred to spiritual or eternal happiness. So we say that a wicked or immoral man can never be really happy, even in this life ; and that even if he could be so, the purchase of it would be a bad investment, as he would only reap eternal misery. It follows then, that that which might be ordered one way with a view to mere temporal happiness, may have to be ordered in another way when the superior end, or the eternal happiness of the subject society is kept in view. Suarez continues: " Et tunc, quamvis temporalis princeps, ejusque potestas in suis actibus directè non pendeat ab aliâ potestate ejusdem ordinis, et quæ eundem finem

---

[1] De Legibus III., cap. v., § 2.

tantùm respiciat; nihilominus fieri potest, ut necesse sit, ipsum dirigi, adjuvari, vel corrigi in suâ materiâ a superiori potestate gubernante homines in ordine ad excellentiorem finem et æternum; et tunc illa dependentia vocatur indirecta, quia illa superior potestas circa temporalia non per se aut propter se, sed quasi indirecte et propter aliud interdum versatur."

The Pope, then, exercises an indirect authority in temporal affairs when he overrules them. Not because he has anything to do with mere politics; but because the ultimate end, of which he has the care, could not be reached by men unless he overruled the means which they employ towards their temporal ends. So, also, the father of a family has a direct authority over his son; and the master over his servant; while the State has an indirect power over both son and servant. "Ergo multo magis Vicarius Christi habet similem potestatem in Reges Christianos, in ordine ad spirituale bonum totius populi Christiani."[1] And St. Thomas Aquinas: "Semper enim invenitur ille, ad quem pertinet ultimus finis, imperare operantibus ea quæ ad finem ultimum ordinantur." In this way, then, the Supreme Pontiff, in aiming at bringing all men to the attainment of the ultimate end of man, must have an indirect power over all the means used by the State—even over those used in aiming at the proximate ends of the State, as they are means to the ultimate end.

It follows, of course, that the correlative—subjection—is also direct and indirect. Direct subjection is that which is within the means and end of the same power or authority. Indirect sub-jection is that which arises from a direction, or governing, or overruling of that power or authority which has the care of an ulterior or higher end, so that the means used by the lower power towards his lower end, may not be repugnant to the attainment of the higher end.

Now, let us arise from the wayside and proceed. Let us look

---

[1] c. xxiii. § 6.

at the matter in this manner. A proprietor, having selected a site on a mountain, determines to build a house. He engages an architect to make the plans of the building, and an engineer to make a road to it, and travels into a far country. The engineer has nothing to say to the question whether the house shall be of Italian or Gothic style; nor may the architect decide whether the road is to be paved or macadamized. But suppose that the engineer lays out the road so as to approach the house on the south side, while the architect has planned the house with the entrance at the north side. Which of the two shall give way to the other? Such a question is always decided by the nobility of their respective ends : the road is made in order to lead to the house ; the house is not built as a graceful termination to the road; therefore the end of the architect is higher than the end of the engineer. In other words, the road is a matter subordinate to the house ; and the engineer is subordinate to the architect. Therefore, in such questions of disputed jurisdiction, the architect has to overrule the engineer. So it is that, in all questions of disputed jurisdiction between Church and State, the Head of the Church must overrule the government of the State. It is, therefore, not an "exorbitant claim," nor is it a "new version of the principles of the Papal Church" which recognises, in the Pontiff, not only a right to "obedience to whatever he may desire, in faith and morals," but also "the right to determine the province of his own rights."[1] It is not an "exorbitant claim," but most rational; nay, a necessity, wherever there is not to be a chaos. Because, as the supreme Pontiff has the care of the highest end of man, his end must necessarily be higher than that of any other power. As Aristotle said: [Pol. vii., 8] πρῶτον ἡ περὶ τῶν θείων ἐπιμέλεια. And as Valerius Maximus [De Relig. i., 1] : " Omnia namque post religionem ponenda, semper noster civitas duxit, etiam in quibus summæ majestatis conspici

---

decus voluit." If you deny the after-life of man, then of course, you must attribute the supremacy to the State. But if man has an eternal life hereafter, the supremacy is undoubtedly in the Church. For clearly, in that case, the life of, say, seventy years on earth, must be subordinate to that life of eternal blessèdness which we hope to live in heaven; and so the particular pleasures, and ends or good things which each man strives after, procures, and enjoys,—and all his riches, learning, mental abilities, health, yea, even life itself, must be in subordination to the end of the highest society, as the only end on account of which these particular good things of earth are sought or enjoyed. And then it follows that "Qui de ultimo fine curam habet, præesse debet his qui curam habent de ordinatis ad finem, et eos dirigere suo imperio." [S. Thom. de Reg. Princ. I., xv.]

Judge from results, if you like. Tell me; is the temporal happiness of the majority in England, or in Germany, or elsewhere, so perfect? Are there no seditions, no Communism, no International? Ah! you are conscious that the State has not even fulfilled its own end since it has discarded the supremacy of the Church. Even antipapal Froude has shown how much better off the poor and the working classes were in Papal times than now. Mr. Thornton proves the same in his book on labour. Or consult Defoe, and see whether he does not give the same testimony. Cobbet does not mince matters in his demonstration of the same truth. So much for the poor and the labouring class,—themselves a majority of the kingdom. Look higher than they, and you will have to tell the same tale. In my lecture in Dublin, I did not "repudiate ancient history" in disproving Mr. Gladstone's reiterated paragraph of offence; I rehearsed a few out of many historical facts from the times when the claims of the Papacy were the most "exorbitant." I showed that there was then a strong and universal power exerted over the lives of all men, to prevent fighting, enmity, immorality, robbery, lawlessness, rebellion, lying, detraction, and every other

D

sin. There was then an Arbitrator between rulers and their people, to prevent oppression as well as sedition; and between all the nations of the earth, to prevent wars, and invasions and violence. Now, the people have no protector, and the rulers have no bridle. The frequency of wars has increased taxation, and the difficulty of living, and has burdened all countries with debt; and so, by reason of the latter, stock-jobbing and swindling has been favoured ; and by reason of the former, the labour question has cropped up, and become the terror of cabinets. The people suffer oppression at home, and are dragged abroad to be wasted on the dire battle-field.

Since we have, in coasting along this subject, happened to touch on oppression and tyranny, just ask yourself : What is tyranny ? A ruler, be he sovereign or parliament, is tyrannical the moment he transgresses the limits of his proper sphere,—the moment he passes over the confines of his rights, and treads on the rights of others,—the moment he meddles in matters which do not concern him. An act of tyranny is an *injury* (departure from right),—an injury done by one who is more powerful than we are. This can be shown by induction,—by an enumeration of all possible kinds of tyranny. For example : it is an act of tyranny for a town-council to interfere in the private affairs of families,—to meddle in anything that belongs to the rule of the head of the family. It is an act of tyranny for a king to command in purely municipal matters. It is also an act of tyranny for a king or parliament to decree laws concerning ecclesiastical or spiritual matters; because these matters are not within the province of royal or parliamentary authority. Thus the Protestant jurisprudent, Böhmer,[1] said : " Graviter pecaret in prima jurisprudentiæ principia, qui res universitatis, vel sacræ vel profanæ (quæ *ex* ejus patrimonio esse dicuntur) iis quæ juris publici sunt, adjungere, vel dominium carum principi vel reipublicæ asserere vellet."

---

[1] Jus Eccles : Potest. III. tit. v. art. 5.

Not only is this true in theory, but also in practice. The only means of preventing abuses of power by a powerful man, is to maintain over him a superior power. But a king is a powerful man. He, therefore, cannot be prevented from falling into the practice of tyranny, except he is regarded as subordinate to a superior authority. Manufacture this safeguard as you like; you must at last rise up to the highest possible human superior—the link between man's rule and God's rule—the connection between a partial ruler and the King of the whole earth. One who is to wield such an immense authority must have been instituted by our Lord, when He came to redeem all society—to redeem all the world; and he must enjoy a supernatural light and judgment from God; nay, the Spirit of Truth must be given to him, to lead him unto all truth, in order that he may lead those under him, and so that the universal society may be led. Such a Supreme Ruler has been provided by our Lord. He is the Ruler of the Universal Commonwealth—of the Catholic Church.

An objection may here be started—a futile objection; but let us notice it! "But then you would limit the King's Sovereignty." Sovereignty must, in the nature of things, be Sovereign, independent, unlimited. But the Sovereign, or King, may have a sphere of action more or less circumscribed. Yes, and your vaunt and glory in England is, that you have a "limited Monarchy." So, then, you do not consider it an evil to limit the King! You circumscribe his action by the caprices of the people and the will of two Chambers! Would it, then, be a greater evil to limit him only by God's law, and by that which is required to enable all his subjects to reach the ultimate end of man —namely, happiness beyond the grave, as well as happiness on this side of it? This is not the same thing as casting a doubt on the character and legitimacy of Sovereignty, as do the Rights-of-man-Liberals, or, at all events, the Revolutionists of '89. When the State restrains a cruel father, it does not thereby deny paternal authority. No more does the Supreme Pontiff, in restraining the illegal, unjust, criminal intentions of a sovereign, deny the divine origin of sovereignty. On the contrary, he says that *because* it is divine in its origin, therefore it can and should be kept within its proper bounds by a divine authority of a superior order. It would be highly illogical to say, "God has made sovereignty, therefore it knows no restraints." But if a king is to be controlled by the law of God, then there must be an interpreter of the law, and judge to declare and execute the law ; and that legislator and judge must be superior to every temporal sovereign.

So, again, the " sacred right of resistance " (as it has been called) on the part of the people, must, at best, be in every case a doubtful right. Whatever theory you may understand by the term, yet every practical and concrete difficulty that arises must be of "such a questionable shape " that it may be impossible to apply the theory. On the other side, we know that St. Paul said, even of Nero : "The powers that be are ordained of God ; whosoever, therefore, resisteth the power, resisteth the ordinance of God." When resistance is urged by some of the people, how can others of the people judge for themselves that it is right to resist ? But if there is a restraining authority of a higher order than that king who is accused of being a tyrant or of oppressing his subjects, then the difficulty vanishes. Then resistance can no longer be a resort to brute power, put in force by the caprices of the mob. It is then an appeal from the king to the law of God. Therefore, it is the support of law and justice, and does not deny sovereignty, nor admit of revolution. There are then called in only reason and submission, not fierce passion and violence. Which, then, is better for both sovereigns and people ? Revolution has never remedied the wrong which had been originally complained of, and has always added a thousand other evils to it ; so that the country, at last, has become and remained for a long time, saddled with countless evils and a much more tyrannical government than before. On the other hand, the Life and Letters of Innocent III. or of Gregory VII., for example, or the Annals of Baronius and Reynaldus furnish numerous instances of the beneficial effects of the judgments of the Supreme Pontiffs.

Furthermore, the superior authority of the Pontiff adds to the majesty of the king. For if the king is to depend on the support and favour of his people alone, he must be guided by them, and even dictated to by them. Sometimes kings, in modern times, have thus been driven into courses which their consciences could not approve. When, on the other hand, the king and people know and feel that there is the Divine Law above both, which both must obey, and both must acknowledge as the one rule of life; and when they are reminded daily that the Law of God will be enforced against them,—then how different are their relations towards each other! Thus, St. Thomas of Aquin, the political philosopher of Christendom, wrote: "Qui favorem hominum quœrit, necesse est ut in omni eo quod dicit aut facit, eorum voluntati deserviat; et sic dum placere hominibus studet, fit servus singulorum."

The king should not look for his reward from the people. His end must not be to be spoken well of by his people. "He is the Minister of God for good." A servant of God must look to God alone for his wages and rewards. "To his master he standeth or falleth." His aim must be to promote the real happiness of his people, by maintaining justice and the Law of God, even to resisting his people when they are lawless. That must be his aim; because he is God's Mandatory or Agent to carry out that end. And every minister of God must seek to be instructed in the Law of God, by the organ of the Church of God. He must look to the Vicar of Christ, as above all terrestrial ministers of God, as being Christ's Vice-regent on earth.

There is another point which requires thought. Legislative Assemblies frequently make laws which are unjust; and "Lex

injusta non est lex." Yet who is to tell the Legislature that it
has passed a statute which is not law ? Let us consider this.
The law of anything is that which renders it apt to attain its end.
Now, man is the only being on earth which has two natures. He
is an animal with an animal nature; and he is likewise made in the
image and likeness of God. Man must therefore have two classes
of ends. The end of the nature which is in the likeness of God,
can be no less than God Himself, the Infinite Good. The other
end is comprised in the order of the world,—the finite good things
of the earth. Happiness in the future life, to be attained by
perfection of the essential powers of man's spiritual nature ; and
happiness in the present time, to be reached by perfection of the
faculties which are used in earthly pursuits. If these are not to
clash, the one must be subordinate to the other;—the latter, of
course, to the former. Just as the part which is in the likeness
of an animal, must be subordinate to the part which is in the
likeness of God,—or the flesh to the soul. The one is the
ultimate end of man ; the other is a partial or proximate end.
Now, natural law imposes means which tend to the ultimate end,
and interdicts all obstacles in the way of it. But suppose that a
statute, passed by a parliament, reverses this, and imposes
obstacles, or forbids means towards the ultimate end ; then that
statute is an " injusta lex," and therefore it is not law. What
authority, then, shall declare that a statute interferes with the
ultimate end of man ? He, of course, who has the care of that
ultimate end.

For, as there are two dominant ends of man, so there are two
great powers which preside over them, and direct men towards
them : the spiritual power, and the civil power ; the ecclesiastical
or sacerdotal authority, and the political authority ; the one
aiming at the preservation and perfection of the spiritual man,
and the other seeking the preservation and perfection of the
physical man. The civil power is ordered to preserve the peace
and security of the State : " Ut quietam et tranquillam vitam

agamus in omni pietate et castitate."[1] The ecclesiatical power
is ordered towards the attainment of eternal life : "Obedite
præpositis[2] vestris, ipsi enim pervigilant tanquam rationem pro
animis vestris reddituri."[3]

Arbitrary government or tyranny occurs where the ruler
steps out of his province, or invades the rights of others. Whenever a government is not subordinate to the law of God, it is
tyrannical.   If, then, we would avoid tyranny, or arbitrary
government, we must take care that the exponent, judge and
executor of the laws relating to man's temporal end, shall be
subordinate to the interpreter, judge, and enforcer of the laws
relating to man's eternal end.   Yet the fundamental position,—
the fundamental error of Liberal politicians, with all their big
bow-wow brag of liberty, is to put the latter out of view
altogether, and to regard the State as the only social power.   In
other words, Liberal government is essentially a tyranny; and
when it is not a tyranny in practice, it is only because the hearts
of the Gladstones are better than their heads.

The way the Liberals get rid of the Church is to forget that
She is a being, which is one, holy, catholic, and Apostolic (as the
Nicene Creed avers).   They imagine the Church to be a mere
voluntary agglomeration of men, without organisation, and without
a common principle of life.   Over such a so-called Church, of
course there cannot be a supreme Pontiff.

Then the High-Church people (who are Liberals;—all "modern
thought" is Liberal) exclaim: "Yes, but the sovereignty shall be
in a 'council,' or parliament of the whole Church."   This would
be, at best, but an intermittent sovereignty (which is a contradiction in terms, and is absurd or impossible in practice).   Besides,
who is to call the bishops of various nations together ?   Who is
to preside over the council ? who is to arrange the order of its
work ? who is to decide how it has judged ? who is to dismiss

---

[1] 1 Tim. ii.   [2] Bishops.   [3] Heb. xiii.

it when it has finished ? who is to proclaim its decisions ? who is to see that its decrees are executed ?

Then the low Church, or Evangelicals (who are also liberals), cry out: "No, the government of the Church shall neither be a monarchy of the Pope, nor an aristocracy of Bishops; but a Republic of the laity or people of the Church." Yet every one knows that a large Republic is no Republic, but is really a monarchy under a ruling person (consisting of one man, or of a body of men, who sit round a green baize table).

Then the Congregationalists (who are Ultra-Liberals) shout out: "Each congregation shall be a separate Church and a separate Republic." But thus there is no longer *one* Church but millions of them; because, *ex hypothesi,* there may be no common Government to rule over the millions. And as the congregations are to rule, they will differ in every place, and vary from time to time; so that this conglomeration will not be *Catholic.* Neither will they be *holy,* nor, of course, *Apostolic;* because the grand and fundamental error of supposing the Church not to be a Being formed of God is, that it makes the Church to depend on the will of men who choose to associate themselves. They are, conversely, equally free to separate themselves whenever they like—a freedom of which Protestants very largely avail themselves. But whatever depends on the will of man cannot be holy (for man's will, like the "imaginations of man's heart," is "only evil continually"); nor yet can it be Apostolic, or framed in the days of the Apostles, and adhering to the Apostolic See. Thus the individualism of Liberalism, and the individualism of Congregationalism, are alike in contradiction to the idea of a Church.

There is a lower depth still, below this depth and bathos of Liberalism. The fundamental error of all is, that the present life is no longer regarded as a means, or as something in subordination to the eternal end of man; but is looked upon as itself the end of man. Then the rational part of man finds its only employment in satisfying the wants of the present life, and ministering to the desires of the flesh. As man is one,—an individual,—although he is of two natures, and of various faculties ; and as he is an intelligent being, therefore he must have only one end which he regards as supreme ; and all his faculties must devise means (or subordinate ends) in subordination to this end, whatsoever it be. The only question, therefore, for us each to ask ourselves, is : What is my end ?

Plato was not so far wrong in his " Politics," when he made Socrates say that the only way to study politics was to study the nature of man ; because that a State is a large image of that of which man is a small image. What do we find in man ? Many members, each of which has its peculiar function ; and yet the action of each member, at every moment, is in subordination to the end which the mind has in view. The mind, too, is of various parts, each of which has its own work ; and yet each part works, at every moment of time, in subordination to the ruling part of the mind. That ruler is properly the reason ; and when the mind is all subordinate to the throne of reason, then all goes well. But when the passions turn reason off her throne, then there are many who would be rulers ; there is no longer subordination ; all is anarchy. There Plato stopped, for Plato was a Pagan. He knew of various ends on earth, which reason could grasp, and he subordinated them to an ultimate end on earth ; he knew not of an eternal end, which his reason did not see ; he knew not of a holy of holies, behind the veil of the temple, where faith has her seat. If he had known this, he would have likened reason to the temporal ruler, who must govern in subordination to the spiritual ruler ; and he would have known of an ultimate end, to which all earthly ends, in their proper subalternation, must be subordinated. Let us, then, sum up the whole question in the words of King David's prayer : " Lord, teach me to know mine end."

WHITEHEAD, MORRIS & LOWE, PRINTERS, LONDON

www.ingramcontent.com/pod-product-compliance
Lightning Source LLC
Chambersburg PA
CBHW022034080426
42733CB00007B/824